THE LIFE OF DR. NICOLE SUTTON –

A JOURNEY THROUGH SHADOWS AND STRUGGLES. WHERE FAITH FOUND FIRE AND A DREAMER FOUND HERSELF.

© 2025 by Dr. Nicole Sutton

All rights reserved.

No part of this book may be reproduced, distributed, transmitted, stored in a retrieval system, or shared in any form or by any means—electronic, mechanical, photocopying, recording, or otherwise—without the prior written permission of the author, except for brief quotations used in reviews or scholarly works.

This book is a work of nonfiction based on the author's life experiences. Names, locations, and identifying details may have been changed to protect the privacy of individuals referenced. Any resemblance to actual persons, living or deceased, is purely coincidental.

The views and experiences expressed in this book are those of the author and are shared for inspirational and educational purposes only. This book is not intended as legal, financial, medical, or professional advice.

Published by:
Twenty Pearls Publishing Co.
Printed in the United States of America
First Edition

ISBN: 979-8-9932163-2-4

THE LIFE OF DR. NICOLE SUTTON

A JOURNEY THROUGH SHADOWS AND STRUGGLES. WHERE FAITH FOUND FIRE AND A DREAMER FOUND HERSELF.

DEDICATION

I dedicate this book to my beloved grandmother, who was always there for me, listening and guiding me through right and wrong. Her love and wisdom remain a constant source of inspiration; I miss her daily.

To my husband, whose unwavering support over the past 26 years has shaped me into the person I am today. Even when it seems like I'm not listening, your encouragement and gentle push have kept me on track. Thank you for always being my anchor.

Lastly, to my wonderful children: you're understanding and support during the times I had to chase my dreams meant the world to me. I appreciate your patience and love while

THE LIFE OF DR. NICOLE SUTTON

I worked to create a better future for us. You know who you are, and I love you dearly.

ACKNOWLEDGEMENTS

I want to express my heartfelt gratitude to the following individuals whose support has been invaluable:

My Husband: You are my best friend and my everything. Thank you for always being there for me and for being open with me about life. Your love and encouragement have made all the difference.

Dallas: My son, my heart, my everything a mom could ask for. You look out for me and always ensure I am happy. I love you so much, son!

My Daughters: To my two beautiful girls, I love you both more than words can say. Although we shouldn't grow up with our kids,

THE LIFE OF DR. NICOLE SUTTON

I've learned so much from you and continue to do so every day. My eldest daughter, you are one of my main reasons for being strong. Thank you both for your love and inspiration.

THE FOREWORD

I'm writing for every woman who grew up in the heart of the struggle—for the girls from the hood, raised by grandparents who gave everything they had, and fathers who showed up in silence but not in presence.

This is for the ones who had to grow up too fast. The ones who knew pain before they knew peace. The ones who carried adult burdens in little girl bodies, but still dared to dream with hands tied by circumstance.

These are my sisters in spirit. The ones who will read these words and say, "She gets it. That's me." But this book is for more than just them.

It's for the people who never had to fight like we did — who need to understand the fire behind our resilience.

I want the world to feel the heartbeat of every overlooked girl who was told she'd never make it. I want women from every background to see what happens when you bet on yourself — even when the world doesn't.

This book is my voice for the voiceless. For the daughters of absence, the carriers of unspoken trauma, the women still looking for healing in places they were told don't exist.

Because this isn't just my story.

It's our story.

THE LIFE OF DR. NICOLE SUTTON

And now we are telling it loudly, boldly, unapologetically.

THE LIFE OF DR. NICOLE SUTTON

Table of Contents

Dedication ii

Acknowledgements vi

The Foreword viii

The Dream That Lit The Fire 16

The Power of Starting Again 31

Lessons The Rain Taught 34

Becoming the Light 36

The Rebirth 38

How to Keep Going When Life Gets Hard 40

Keep Walking Through the Rain 48

When Life Got Real 51

The Breaking That Built Me 68

Healing the Little Girl in Me 71

Becoming the Author of My Life 74

Redefining Success 76

The Power of Stillness 78

How to Keep Going When Life Feels Hard 79

For You The Reader 82

The Hustle That Heals 85

The Turning Point 95

When Success Feels Heavy 97

Redefining Strength 99

Motherhood and Legacy 101

The Woman I Became 103

Faith My Process	105
Purpose Over Popularity	107
Peace, Not Performance	108
How to Keep Going When Life Gets Hard	110
Just For YOU.	113
Why I Keep Going	116
The Morning After Rock Bottom	122
The Climb That Changed Everything	124
The Power of Purpose	126
Becoming THE Example	128
Love, the Quiet Fuel	130
The Reality Behind the Hustle	131
Redefining Success	133
Healing the Inner Child	134
Looking Forward	135
How to Keep Going When Life Gets Hard	136
Just For YOU.	139
Becoming the Brand	142
Becoming The Vision	144
From "Rich Girl" to WhiteApple Financial	146
The Evolution of a Brand	147
Starting a Business from Nothing	150
Handling Business, Not Hustling	152
Professionalism: The Language of Success	153
From Hustling to Handling Business	155

Sacrifice and Self-Mastery.. 157
The Weight of Responsibility 159
The Reality of Growth 162
Legacy Over Lifestyle... 164
The Woman Behind the Brand 166
Lessons for Those Ready to Build Something from Nothing 167
Just for YOU. 170
The Power of Saying No 173
When "No" Becomes Your Superpower................... 176
The Year of Tough Love - 2025 178

THE LIFE OF DR. NICOLE SUTTON

CHAPTER ONE

THE LIFE OF DR. NICOLE SUTTON

The Dream That Lit The Fire

What dream did I have when I was a little child?

Even now, that question takes me back. I don't remember the details — not the exact age, not the day — but I do remember the feeling. I always had this dream… this quiet belief that life could be better than what I saw around me. I didn't grow up with much, but I had imagination. I saw people on TV with nice things. Families that smiled. Kids who didn't have to make jokes about what little they had just to survive emotionally. And I thought, one day, maybe that could be me.

THE LIFE OF DR. NICOLE SUTTON

Where I come from, you make fun of whatever you can get your hands on — your clothes, your shoes, even your dreams. It's how we cope. But behind the jokes and the laughs, I was just a kid hoping for more. Not more stuff, necessarily. More love. More peace. More understanding. I didn't know exactly what it would look like, but I knew I wanted to grow up and have a better life.

And that dream — soft but steady — stayed with me.

My earliest memories carved deep grooves in who I became. I watched people live in different ways. Some kids got hugs and home-cooked meals. Some had both parents, some didn't. Some were treated like gold. Others —

like me — felt like shadows in their own homes.

I didn't talk about it much back then. To be honest, I didn't really know how to. But I felt the difference. I was treated differently. And though I've grown and found reasons to understand some of it… deep down, I still don't know why. All I know is this:

I didn't want to carry that pain forward.

I wanted my future kids to be treated the same — with equal love, no matter what. I didn't want them to feel invisible or less than. I wanted to break the cycle. I wanted to create a home with love at its center — not just for show, but for real.

For most of my childhood, I didn't really know who I was.

I didn't have the space, the guidance, or even the safety to discover myself. Growing up, I just moved through life — adapting, surviving, blending in, doing what I thought I was supposed to do. I never had the chance to pause and ask, "Who am I, really?" The person I was back then... isn't me anymore. Not even close.

I remember one night I was at home and my sister was helping me do my homework and my mom was on phone with my Aunt (her sister). Then my dad walks in house pissed about something to this day I don't know what he was mad about. I remember him standing over my mom, getting the lamp off the table she was sitting by, and starting beating her in the head. That the day my life changed forever. After what happened to my mom, I felt like love disappeared from my life. It wasn't until I got older that I realized I did have family who loved me — they just didn't know how to show it or say it. After that happened to my mom, we bounced from place to place for a while. For a time, we lived with my aunt, and I hated it — the new school, the new house rules, all of it. Nothing felt like home. After we left there, the memories blur, but I remember living with my grandmother starting around second grade. On weekends, I'd go to my mom's house because she worked nights, and those visits were the closest thing I had to feeling normal again. Staying with my grandmother, it was me, my sister, and my uncle all in a small two-bedroom place. My grandmother did the best she could for us, and I'll always be grateful for that.

Still, I seemed to get in trouble almost every day — it felt like I couldn't do anything right back then.

When I got to middle school, I moved back in with my mom full-time. I was happy to be with her again. She was working during the day then, but after I moved in, she had to switch to part-time just to keep the household going because my dad had just gotten out of prison himself. It wasn't easy for her — she never said much about it, but I could see the struggle in her eyes.

As I got older, I started to grow into a young woman with a nice shape, and in high school, my mom often had different men around, moving in and out of our lives. It made things complicated, but I kept pushing forward. I ended up graduating early — in 1998 instead of 1999 — from Lincoln High School in Sunny South Dallas.

By the time I was in beauty school, almost ready to graduate, life took another turn — I got pregnant by a liar. He was married and used me, and at 19 I found myself with my first child, lost and unsure of what to do. I just took it day by day, learning as I went. My grandmother, the woman who had raised me, helped me with my daughter as much as she could until my baby turned one.

Not long after, someone I had known for years — a man who had always been around but I'd never really noticed — started talking to me. I opened up to him and told him my story, and from that moment on, we've never been apart. He came into my life and changed my mind and heart. He taught me what real love feels like, and most of all, he showed me how to forgive my parents.

One core memory that I think still pinch my heart till this day is when my dad didn't come to my high school graduation, I didn't have an extra ticket for his girlfriend at time and when

I got married he didn't show up as well my uncle (his brother in law) was the one who walks me down the aisle.

When in comes to forgiveness, I never forgave my mom because right after I had my first child, her live-in boyfriend kept coming on to me. My best friend saw it, my aunt saw it, and even my mom's cousin saw it — everyone did, except her. She was too busy saying,

"Y'all don't know what she might have done to make him act like that." Hearing that from my own mother — instead of her protecting me, instead of believing me — hurt more than I can ever explain.

At the end of the day, my husband showed me how to forgive and let go. He has been the best thing that ever came into my life, along with our children and grandson. I truly believe I wouldn't have made it this far without him, because he helped me break the cycle in my family. He came from a two-parent home where love was shown and work was valued, and he taught me how to bring that same love and stability into our family. Together, we've passed that on to our kids.

That journey toward becoming better — more whole — meant I had to unlearn a lot. One of the biggest things? I had to stop thinking I needed other people's approval to grow. That included friends, family, even social media. I had to silence the outside noise and finally, finally start listening to myself.

So I did. I tuned everything out. I stopped watching TV. I stepped back from the online world. And I started studying — not just books, but me. I studied my habits. My pain. My triggers. My patterns. I started paying attention to what lifted me up and what tore me down.

It was hard. Lonely, even. But for the first time, I was giving myself a chance to heal. I was doing the work.

And in that quiet, I realized something powerful: I was enough all along. I just needed to believe it.

I used to think growing meant getting stronger on the outside. Now I know: it starts on the inside. It's not about proving anything to anyone. It's about becoming someone you're proud to be — even when no one's watching.

That dream I had as a little kid? It wasn't just some naive wish. It was a promise. One I made to myself a long time ago.

And now?

I'm keeping it.

My childhood reminds me of a story — one that I think lives in all of us. It's the story of a writer who once had nothing. No support system, no money, no audience waiting for her words. Just a dream. Just a tiny spark of belief that maybe, somehow, she could make something of her pain.

THE LIFE OF DR. NICOLE SUTTON

Her path wasn't perfect. In fact, it was full of detours, mistakes, and nights when she questioned everything. She stumbled, again and again, tripping over the same doubts, walking barefoot through storms that most people never saw. She had wounds that didn't always bleed but still hurt. She had dreams that felt too big for her small beginnings.

But you know what she did?

She kept going.

She kept writing, even when the words came out broken.

She kept showing up, even when no one clapped.

She kept fighting for a life she couldn't yet see, trusting that somewhere ahead, the sun would find her again.

That writer could be anyone — maybe me, maybe you, maybe the version of you that still believes there's more out there. Because the truth is, we all carry a story that could have ended in the dark. But something inside us — that quiet, stubborn, beautiful spark — refuses to give up.

That's what healing feels like sometimes. It's not loud. It's not quick. It's not perfect. It's waking up on the days you want to stay under the covers.

It's whispering, "I'll try again tomorrow," when everything in you says you can't. It's walking through the rain with tired feet and a weary heart — but still walking.

The rain doesn't stop her. It washes her. It teaches her. It softens the soil of her life so that something new can grow.

And eventually, it does.

The Power of Starting Again

There's a sacred beauty in starting again — in rebuilding yourself piece by piece after everything fell apart. The world often celebrates the finish line but rarely talks about the strength it takes just to get up and start walking again.

We don't talk enough about the courage it takes to rebuild your confidence after failure. We don't talk enough about the faith it takes to love again after heartbreak. We don't talk enough about the discipline it takes to believe in yourself when no one else does.

But that's where the real growth happens —
not when everything is perfect, but when you
choose to keep going through the mess.

The writer in this story learned that life doesn't
wait for you to be ready. It just keeps moving,
and you have to move with it. She learned that
healing isn't something you "finish." It's
something you live. Every day. Every choice.
Every breath.

When you decide to start again, you reclaim
your power. You stop being a victim of your
past and become the author of your future.
You begin to write a new chapter — one filled
with resilience, purpose, and self-worth.

Starting again means forgiving yourself for not
knowing better before. It means letting go of

who you thought you should be and embracing who you're becoming.

It means realizing that growth doesn't always look like progress — sometimes it looks like rest, reflection, or saying no.

The writer didn't rebuild her life overnight. It took years of discipline, faith, and self compassion. Some days she wanted to quit. Some days she did. But she always came back. Because once you've tasted your potential — once you've seen that there's more to life than just surviving — you can never go back to the version of yourself that settled.

Lessons The Rain Taught

The rain became her teacher. It reminded her that no matter how dark the sky gets, the storm will always pass. The rain told her that growth doesn't happen under sunshine alone — it happens when the soil of your soul is broken open.

She learned that pain can be purposeful. That heartbreak can redirect you to something better. That rejection can be protection. That endings can be beginnings in disguise.

And maybe that's what life is — a series of storms that shape you into who you're meant to become.

Each raindrop carries a lesson:

- That discomfort is often the birthplace of wisdom.

- That faith grows strongest when you can't see the next step.

- That every time you break, you rebuild stronger.

She began to see that her story wasn't just hers — it was a bridge for others to cross. Her pain became someone else's comfort.

Her scars became someone else's survival guide.

Her resilience became a reminder that no one is alone in their healing. And through that, she found purpose.

Becoming the Light
One day, she looked around and realized she wasn't standing in the storm anymore. The rain had stopped. The clouds had cleared. And though she was tired, she was still standing — stronger, wiser, and softer than before.

That's the thing about survival — it doesn't leave you the same. You become someone new. Someone who's no longer afraid of the rain because you've seen what it grows.

The woman she became was no longer chasing perfection or approval. She was chasing peace. She was chasing purpose. She was chasing the freedom that comes from living authentically — unfiltered, unafraid, and unapologetic.

She realized that the light she had been searching for all along wasn't out there — it was within her. It had been shining through her cracks the entire time.

And when she finally saw that, she stopped hiding. She stopped apologizing for being too much or too little. She stopped shrinking to fit into spaces that couldn't hold her truth.

She understood that her journey — every painful, messy, beautiful part of it — was her divine assignment.

Because sometimes, God doesn't change your situation right away. He changes you first. He strengthens your heart, refines your spirit, and prepares you for what's next.

The Rebirth
The writer's story became one of rebirth.

She stopped waiting for the "right moment" to live her life. She realized that healing doesn't mean you have to forget what happened — it means you finally make peace with it.

She learned to thank her past, not curse it.

She learned to love her scars, not hide them.

She learned that being "broken" didn't mean she was unworthy — it meant she was human.

Every morning, she would wake up and whisper, "Thank you." Not because life was perfect, but because she finally saw the beauty in imperfection.

She learned that the hardest battles are often fought in silence. That sometimes, survival looks like getting up, making coffee, and choosing to try again.

She realized that real success isn't about money, followers, or recognition. It's about peace — the kind that lets you sleep at night knowing you're living true to yourself.

She found joy in simplicity. She found strength in solitude. And she found love — real love — by learning to love herself first.

And when people asked her how she made it through, she said:

"Because I refused to stop walking — even in the rain."

How to Keep Going When Life Gets Hard

Here's what the writer — and life — taught me:

No matter how heavy it gets, you can make it through. You just have to know how to keep going even when everything in you wants to stop.

Below are truths, practices, and mindsets that help you stay grounded, even in your hardest seasons.

1. Let yourself feel everything.

Healing doesn't mean pretending to be strong all the time. It means allowing yourself to cry, to be angry, to grieve. Feelings are not weaknesses — they are messages. Every emotion has something to teach you.

The more you avoid your pain, the longer it controls you. But the moment you face it, it starts to lose its power.

2. Remember your "why."

When life feels unbearable, go back to your purpose — the reason you started. Maybe it's your children. Maybe it's your future self. Maybe it's the dream that won't let you go. Your "why" will hold you when motivation fails.

3. Rest doesn't mean quitting.

You're allowed to take breaks. Rest is part of the process, not a sign of weakness. Even flowers close at night — that doesn't mean they've stopped growing.

When you rest, you reset. And when you reset, you return stronger.

4. Speak kindly to yourself.

Self-talk can be medicine or poison. Replace "I can't" with "I'm learning." Replace "I failed" with "I tried."

You can't build a peaceful life with a mind full of self-criticism.

Talk to yourself the way you would talk to someone you love.

5. Keep showing up.

You don't need to have it all figured out. Just keep moving. Keep showing up — for your dreams, your healing, your growth.

Progress isn't about perfection; it's about persistence.

Some days, showing up looks like winning. Other days, it looks like surviving. Both count.

6. Surround yourself with truth-tellers, not comforters.

You need people who don't just tell you what you want to hear, but what you need to hear. People who challenge you to grow, who remind you of your strength, who don't let you stay small.

Healing requires honesty — and community built on truth.

7. Forgive — not for them, but for you.

Forgiveness isn't approval. It's release.

It's choosing not to let old pain take up new space in your life. You don't need to reconnect, but you do need to let go.

Because holding onto resentment is like drinking poison and expecting someone else to die.

8. Don't compare your chapter to someone else's.

Your pace is not too slow. Your story is not too late.

Everyone blooms in their own season.

Comparison will steal your peace faster than failure ever could.

Stay in your lane and trust your process.

9. Keep faith — even when it's quiet.

Faith isn't always loud and confident. Sometimes it's a whisper: "I don't know how, but I'll keep going."

That's enough.

Faith is walking when you can't see the finish line — and trusting that every step matters.

10. Turn your pain into purpose.

Whatever you've gone through, use it. Let it fuel your growth. Let it guide someone else. There's power in saying, "I survived — and now I'll help others survive too."

Your story isn't just your pain. It's your legacy.

11. Choose gratitude daily.

Even when life feels impossible, there's always something to be thankful for — a breath, a sunrise, a lesson. Gratitude doesn't erase the pain, but it reminds you that you still have reasons to hope.

12. Be patient with your becoming.

You're not supposed to have it all figured out right now.

Healing takes time. Growth takes time.

You're becoming the person your younger self prayed for — and that takes grace.

13. Protect your peace.

Not everyone deserves access to your energy. Choose who gets close to you. Set boundaries without guilt. You don't owe anyone your peace.

Peace is sacred — guard it like it's gold.

14. Believe in your comeback.

You've already survived your worst days. That means you're capable of so much more than you think.

Every setback is a setup for a stronger version of you.

Your story isn't over — it's just unfolding.

Keep Walking Through the Rain
Life will test you. It will break you open. But remember — that's how light gets in. You are not defined by what hurt you, but by how you choose to rise from it.

The rain might fall, the road might get muddy, and your feet might ache — but keep walking.

Because on the other side of the storm, the sun will rise again.

And when it does, you'll realize something powerful:

You were never just surviving.

You were growing.

You were blooming.

You were becoming.

And that — that is your miracle.

Chapter Two

When Life Got Real
I didn't start finding myself until about five years ago. And when I did, it was like waking up from a long, exhausting sleep. I looked around and thought, This is who I am. This is who I've always been — and nobody can take that from me.

That moment of clarity felt like breathing real air for the first time.

The truth is, life taught me early on that it wasn't going to hand me anything. The moment that truth hit hardest? When I had my first daughter.

When I realized I didn't have a permanent place for me and my daughter to stay. I had to leave my mom's house because she didn't believe me about her boyfriend hitting on me at the time. I went to her cousin's house and stayed there for about a week, but then I left. After that, I went back to my mom's house for about two weeks. When things didn't work out there either, I moved out again — and me and my daughter ended up living in my car. I used to go back and forth between both of my grandmothers' houses to have a place to sleep. They both lived in South Dallas. Some days I'd stay at my mom's house, and other days I'd stay at my dad's mom's house. I remember one day, my grandmother — my dad's mother — told me that my dad had said she needed to kick me out of her house, I was heartbroken. I told my husband (My husband now, but at the time he wasn't really my husband yet) "I have nowhere to go — it's just me and my daughter." With a big heart he told me to move in with him. I moved in with him, and around that time I started working a night job. One of my uncle's friends began helping me by watching my daughter at night. During the day, I would try to get some sleep and still do hair to make a little extra money. It was very hard for me — I was a mother, living with someone, trying to work and take care of my daughter, all while trying not to be in his space or in his way and be a burden to him. Eventually, I started leaving more often, thinking I could find somewhere else to stay.

At that time, I had just finished beauty school. I decided to step out on faith and start working at the beauty salon full-time. So, I quit my other job and began focusing completely on doing hair. That way, I could spend more time with my daughter and build up my clientele. I hadn't yet taken my state board licensing test, so I wasn't licensed. The salon took a chance on me, trusting that I would get my license soon — and my boyfriend (now my husband), supported me through it all.

He took me to get ready to go to Austin to take my licensing test, but as we were leaving, I got nervous and told him to turn around. He tried his best to talk me into going, but I couldn't do it — I was too scared. So I kept working without a license and ended up doing hair for 17 years that way. Ironically, the year I finally decided to get my license was also the year I chose to stop doing hair. I got my license and transitioned into becoming a lash tech. But before that, I went through so many bumps and bruises just trying to get where I wanted to be. It often felt like I was forced to stay with my boyfriend because I had nowhere else to go. I just wanted a place that felt safe and comfortable for me and my daughter. And even though I truly did care for him, a part of me knew I was also holding on out of survival, felt like I am just there because he held out his hands for me out of kindness.

I couldn't believe that a man like him would want to be with a broken woman who had nothing. It was hard because I didn't even know myself. I was trying to find out who I was while learning how to be a new mother, someone's partner, and an entrepreneur all at once. I had so many headaches and moments of confusion because I was still searching for the woman I wanted to become. Life kept moving forward for us, even when I felt lost. Then one day, I got a phone call from my mom saying I had some mail from Section 8. I went to her house to pick it up — and sure enough, it was real. It was a letter from Section 8 telling me that I had been approved for a housing voucher. I couldn't believe it. When I first applied for Section 8, it wasn't even for me — a friend had asked me to take her to apply. When we got there, she realized she had left her ID and Social Security card at home. The lady at the office looked at me and said, "Ma'am, I can see it in your face — you need this help. Do you have your ID and Social

Security card with you?" I told her, "Yes, ma'am, but I only brought my friend here to apply." She said, "Then you need to apply too." So I did. I had no idea at that moment that what felt like a simple act of kindness would turn into one of the biggest blessings for me and my daughter in the years to come.

I wasn't looking for a handout, but that handout turned out to be a blessing I truly needed. I had been living with my boyfriend for about six months before my housing came through. When I found out I got approved, I felt so guilty. I went to talk to my grandmother and said, "Mama, I got a housing voucher, but I don't know how to tell him that me and my daughter are going to leave. We've gotten used to each other." She told me, "He helped you when you needed a place to stay, so you need to be honest with him and let him know." So I did. I told him, and he understood. We worked everything out. I stayed on Section 8 for about three years, and during that time I worked my way up. I got a job at a serious company working on washers and dryers, and I stayed there for about two years — until I found out I was pregnant with my son.

After I got pregnant with my son, I decided to quit my job because it was getting too hard on my body. I told myself it was time to take my business seriously and go full-time in the hair industry. I had two babies now — not just one — and I needed to make things work. So I went all in with my business and never looked back. Eventually, I was able to get off Section

8, and we moved into a family home. At first, everything was good, and we built our life there. But we ended up staying in that house for 17 years. After all that time, the main person who owned the home told us we had to move out — and they didn't give us much time. That was another really hard moment in my life. We went from paying no rent to suddenly having just four weeks to come up with $4,000 for a new place.

So I did. I told him, and he understood. We worked everything out. I stayed on Section 8 for about three years, and during that time I worked my way up. I got a job at a serious company working on washers and dryers, and I stayed there for about two years — until I found out I was pregnant with my son.

THE LIFE OF DR. NICOLE SUTTON

When I found out, I decided to quit because the job was hard on my body. I told myself it was time to take my business seriously. I had two babies now, not just one, and I needed to make it work. I went full-time in the hair business and never looked back. Eventually, I was able to get off Section 8, and we moved into a family home. Everything was good for a while. We built our life there and stayed for 17 years. But after all that time, the main person who owned the house told us we had to move out — and they didn't give us much time. That was another tough moment in my life. We went from paying nothing to having just four weeks to come up with $4,000 for a new place.

That's when I told myself, I'll never put myself in that kind of predicament again. I'll never let anyone else have control over my life. From that day forward, I decided to take full control of my journey.

Life will always have its ups and downs. No matter how good things seem, something will always come along to test you — to humble you and remind you to be thankful. So I've learned to be grateful every single day. There are people who want to be in your shoes, but they don't want to go through the bumps and bruises it takes to get there. I've been through those bumps and bruises. I know what it's like to have nothing — nowhere to sleep, no money, having to ask for help, to sit in the Section 8 and food stamp offices. But I also know what it feels like to finally say, "I'm blessed — I don't need it anymore."

From that moment on, I never worked a "regular job" again. I built a life where I worked for myself — and I never looked back.

I started putting myself out there. Telling people about my work. Building a client base from scratch. And I kept showing up. Every. Single. Day. And something amazing happened — I built it. One braid, one style, one word-of-mouth referral at a time.

Because I had seen what it was like to be limited by someone else's paycheck. Working 9 to 5, barely scraping by. I told myself: If I can grind for someone else's dream, I can sure as hell grind for my own.

Those early struggles? They didn't break me.

They built me.

THE LIFE OF DR. NICOLE SUTTON

Years ago, I was struggling so hard in life I was what you'd call a "yes girl." I wanted to help everyone, please everyone, be liked by everyone. I let people take and take — my time, my energy, my kindness. But pain teaches you things. People will use you if you let them. And eventually, I had to stop saying yes to everyone and start saying yes to me.

Now? I say no. And I don't feel guilty for it.

Because everyone has a story. Everyone has pain. Everyone has a book inside them. But what matters is what you do with your story. Are you just going to keep telling it from a place of pain? Or are you going to write a new chapter — one where you become the hero?

That's what I chose. And that choice made me stronger. Wiser. More in control of my emotions. I'm not that same soft-spoken girl anymore. I have boundaries. I have purpose. I know who I am now — and I protect her at all costs.

Then came the moment that changed everything. This is my ups after the downs COVID.

At the time, I was doing eyelash extensions. That was my only source of income. And when the world shut down, so did my business. It was scary. One day I was making money daily — and the next, nothing. I had savings, but even that started to run out after months without work.

So I did what I always do when my back is against the wall — I pivoted. I got into taxes.

It started as an idea — What if I could offer services without my clients ever needing to come in? That way, I could work from anywhere, anytime, and still support my people. I leaned in. I trained. I got certified. And eventually, I was referred and known as Dr. NiCole Sutton and founded the Rich Girl Brand LLC now known as WhiteApple Financial Company.

That's when I knew: this wasn't the end of my hustle. It was just a new direction. They say pressure makes diamonds. I believe that.

Because every struggle I faced — every no, every loss, every long night — shaped me into a woman who's not afraid to bet on herself.

There were so many nights when I cried silently, not because I was weak, but because I was tired of being strong all the time. I used to ask, "Why me? Why do I always have to struggle so hard?" And the answer that came years later was this: because I was being prepared. Prepared to handle the things I hoped for.

It's easy to live life when things are good. But when life knocks you down, when the rent's due, when the car breaks down, when you're trying to hold your family together while holding yourself together — that's when you know life gets real. That's when you find out who you truly are.

I didn't realize it then, but every closed door, every betrayal, every sleepless night was molding me. Teaching me to trust myself. To listen to my own voice.

I remember a time when my biggest dream was simply having stability — a home that was mine, a business that was steady, and peace that wasn't temporary. I didn't want luxury. I just wanted peace.

But peace, I learned, doesn't come from circumstances. It comes from within.

The Breaking That Built Me
When we finally moved out of that house after seventeen years, I was devastated. It felt like losing everything we built — all the memories, all the laughter, the roots we had planted. I felt like I was being thrown back into the unknown.

But here's the thing about starting over: it reminds you how capable you are.

Moving forced me to reorganize not just my home, but my life. I learned that sometimes, God removes us from comfort to remind us that we still have more to grow into. I stopped viewing that loss as punishment and started seeing it as redirection.

Because when you've been through enough storms, you stop asking "why me?" and start saying "try me."

I started setting new goals — bigger ones. Not just financial, but spiritual and emotional. I wanted to be intentional about my peace. I started journaling daily. I began waking up early just to sit in silence before the world got loud. I told myself: You're no longer surviving. You're rebuilding.

And rebuilding meant doing things differently.

It meant learning that not everyone deserves access to me.

It meant saying "no" without apology.

It meant not letting fear make my choices.

THE LIFE OF DR. NICOLE SUTTON

Because fear had controlled too much of my life — fear of failing, fear of being alone, fear of not being enough. But once you've lost everything and rebuilt from scratch, you realize you have nothing left to fear.

Healing the Little Girl in Me

You know, the hardest part of healing isn't forgiving others — it's forgiving yourself.

For years, I carried guilt. Guilt for staying in situations too long. Guilt for not knowing better. Guilt for letting people hurt me. But one day, I sat down with myself and said, "You did the best you could with what you knew at the time."

That's when I started healing the little girl in me — the one who never felt safe, the one who thought love had to hurt, the one who always tried to prove her worth.

I told her, "You're safe now. You don't have to beg anyone to choose you."

And slowly, I started showing up differently. My energy shifted. I became more selective about who I allowed near me. I stopped chasing love and started nurturing self-love.

I realized that when you love yourself the way you wanted others to love you, you stop settling for half-hearted connections. You stop trying to fix people who broke themselves. You stop shrinking to make others comfortable.

Healing isn't pretty — it's messy, it's uncomfortable, it's lonely at times. But it's worth every tear.

Because when you heal, you break generational patterns. You show your children what strength looks like. You teach them that it's okay to fall apart, as long as you keep

putting yourself back together.

Becoming the Author of My Life

There came a day when I stopped waiting for validation. I stopped explaining myself to people who didn't understand my journey.

I realized that every time I dimmed my light to make others comfortable, I was betraying myself.

So I stopped.

I became the author of my own story. Literally and spiritually.

Writing became my release — my way of reclaiming my voice. For so long, I had swallowed my pain in silence. But when I started writing it down, I realized my story wasn't just mine — it was medicine for someone else.

That's why I decided to share it. Because someone out there is sleeping in their car tonight. Someone out there feels unseen and unheard. Someone out there is wondering if their life will ever get better. And if my story can give them even a flicker of hope, then everything I went through was worth it.

Because the truth is, I didn't go through hell just to keep quiet about it. I went through it so I could help someone else find their way out.

Redefining Success

For a long time, I thought success was about money, cars, and homes. But I've learned that true success is being able to sleep at night knowing you stayed true to yourself.

It's being able to look in the mirror and love the person staring back at you. It's about peace. Freedom. Joy.

These days, I measure success differently. Success is being able to say no without guilt. It's walking away from what no longer serves me. It's choosing myself every single day — even when it's uncomfortable.

I used to think I needed to be everything for everyone — the perfect mother, the perfect partner, the perfect entrepreneur. But now I know I just need to be present. To show up authentically. To live from a place of love, not fear.

Because I am no longer that woman trying to prove her worth.

I am the woman who knows her worth.

The Power of Stillness
One of the most powerful lessons I've learned is that growth doesn't always happen in motion. Sometimes it happens in stillness.

For years, I kept myself busy — thinking if I kept moving, I wouldn't have to feel. But slowing down forced me to face myself. To listen to my thoughts. To unlearn the habits that were keeping me stuck.

Stillness became my strength. It taught me that peace is not found in noise, but in alignment.

When you learn to be still, you stop chasing — you start attracting. You start drawing in opportunities, relationships, and blessings that are meant for you because you're finally aligned with who you are.

How to Keep Going When Life Feels Hard

Here are a few truths I've learned through every season of pain, faith, and growth:

1. Let yourself feel.

Don't rush your healing. Pain demands to be felt so it can teach you something. Numbness only delays growth.

2. Don't compare your journey.

You can't measure your path by someone else's highlight reel. You're not late — you're right on time for your story.

3. Rest isn't weakness.

Rest is repair. You don't have to earn your right to slow down. Even flowers need darkness to bloom again.

4. Learn to pivot, not quit.

When one door closes, another opens — but you have to be willing to shift directions. Adaptability is power.

5. Protect your peace.

Not everyone deserves access to your energy. Guard it like it's sacred — because it is.

6. Forgive without needing closure.

Forgiveness is freedom. It's not about them; it's about releasing yourself from the chains of resentment.

7. Be proud of small wins.

Progress isn't always loud. Sometimes it's just waking up and trying again. That's courage.

8. Speak life into yourself.

Your words are seeds. Plant ones that grow healing, not harm. Tell yourself daily: I'm worthy, I'm capable, I'm enough.

9. Surround yourself with faith-filled people.

Energy is contagious — so sit at tables where love, growth, and grace are served.

10. Never forget who you are.

Even when life shakes you, remember: your value doesn't decrease because of a hard season. You're still chosen. You're still powerful. You're still you.

For You The Reader

If you're reading this and you're in a dark place right now — please don't give up. I know you're tired.

I know it feels like you've been fighting forever.

But I promise, the version of you that's waiting on the other side of this pain will thank you for not quitting.

You might not see it now, but every storm is shaping you.

Every disappointment is redirecting you.

Every heartbreak is strengthening you.

Keep going. You are not behind. You are not broken. You are becoming.

THE LIFE OF DR. NICOLE SUTTON

Every chapter of your life — even the painful ones — is part of your purpose. You are not your mistakes. You are not your past. You are a walking testimony of what survival looks like when it turns into strength.

You've made it through 100% of your hardest days.

And that means you're undefeated.

So keep going. Keep growing.

Because the story isn't over yet — it's just beginning.

Chapter Three

The Hustle That Heals

Here's one thing I promised myself a long time ago...

I will never be homeless again.

That was one of the lowest points in my life — not having a place to call home. I remember going from couch to couch, staying with friends, and sometimes even sleeping in a car with my clothes packed in the trunk. I was young, and maybe I didn't fully understand how deep that pain went. But as I got older, the reality of it hit me harder. That version of life? That feeling of instability and uncertainty? I made a vow — I'd never go back to that. Not ever.

I realized that it was only me who truly cared about me — and if I didn't make a change, things would only get worse. So, I took time to think fast, because at that moment, I couldn't afford to move slow. I was already in a bad place. Looking back, I feel like I had to go through that to become who I am now. If I hadn't experienced that pain, I don't think I'd appreciate the life I have today — with my husband and family.

I built myself a whole new family, because I learned something powerful: the family you're born into isn't always the family you have to stay with. But you can control who you build your family with. And I love mine. We've had more bad days than good ones, but we grew through them together. Now, I'm proud to say we have more joy, more peace, and more gratitude than ever before.

Through growth, I've learned to talk to the younger generation — especially the young women coming up behind me. I try to guide them, tell them which route to take, but sometimes they don't listen. Maybe it's because, like me, they have to fall hard to truly understand. I didn't have anyone to walk me through life lessons either. I grew up seeing things that weren't right, things I had to unlearn on my own.

So if I can help any young lady, I'd tell her this:

Follow your heart — for yourself, not for anyone else. If you ever get forced to move fast, think fast and smart, but on your own time. Don't tell everyone your dreams, because not everyone will be happy for you, no matter how they act. Some people will smile in your face but close doors behind your back. So keep your head high. Walk with grace. Let your energy speak for you when you enter a room — because true strength and good character always shine through.

And that's why I work so hard.

Some people clock in for a paycheck. I wake up every day fueled by the memory of what it felt like to have nothing. That kind of hunger doesn't fade — it drives you. It pushes you. It makes you climb until you can't see the ground anymore.

THE LIFE OF DR. NICOLE SUTTON

I work in a client-based business, which means I serve people — and people come with expectations. Some days, no matter how much you give, not everyone will be satisfied. But I still give it my all. Because I know that I'm not just working for today's praise —

I'm working for my future. I'm working to prove to my kids that they don't have to clock in for someone else if they don't want to. They can build something from their passion. They can create freedom through what they love.

I tell them, If you wouldn't do it for free, it's not your purpose.

People ask me all the time, "How do you work so hard?"

THE LIFE OF DR. NICOLE SUTTON

Here's how: I sacrifice.

I don't go out when I'm invited. I skip shopping trips, club nights, movie dates, and random weekend plans. I miss out on a lot of what people call "fun." And to be honest? I don't miss it at all.

My day starts early — I wake up, work out, and head straight into my business. I work. And then I work some more. I pour myself into what I do.

From January through May — my busiest season — I might get just one or two hours of sleep. That's it. I'm that committed. And you know what? I love it.

I take classes constantly, improving my skills, learning more, preparing for the next opportunity. Because when it's time to show up for my clients, I want to be at my best. I don't believe in doing anything halfway — especially not when it comes to the life I'm building for my family.

This isn't just a job to me. It's my mission.

Looking back, the hardship I faced gave me something I never would've learned in comfort: a positive outlook on hard work.

Whether you work for yourself or someone else, one thing is guaranteed — you will have to work. There's no way around it. But the way I see it, working for what you have is something to be proud of. It's not just about having money; it's about the dignity and freedom that comes with earning it.

Paying my own bills. Taking care of my kids. Never having to ask anyone for anything — that's what makes me feel strong. That's what makes me feel whole. So yes, I work hard. And I feel good about it.

At one point in my life, I believed success looked like fame, money, luxury — all the external stuff people like to post on social media. But as I've grown, I've unlearned that belief.

Now I know that real success is about fulfillment.

It's about doing what you love, creating something that lasts, and waking up proud of the life you're living. It's about building relationships that are genuine and finding peace with who you are — not just what you have. And once you understand that, your whole perspective shifts.

You stop chasing validation and start creating value.

You stop living for applause and start living with purpose.

You stop surviving — and start thriving.

Sometimes, I look around my home — the laughter, the love, the stillness — and I think about that girl I used to be. The one who was scared, uncertain, trying to hold everything together when everything was falling apart.

If I could sit across from her now, I'd hold her hand and tell her, "You made it. You're safe now. You can breathe."

Because for so long, I didn't breathe. Not really. I was always bracing myself for the next fall, the next loss, the next heartbreak. I thought if I could just work harder, stay busy, or keep people happy, I could finally feel secure.

But life doesn't work that way. Security isn't built from approval — it's built from alignment.

And the moment I realized that, everything began to shift.

The Turning Point

When I said I'd never be homeless again, I didn't just mean having a roof over my head. I meant I'd never let myself feel spiritually or emotionally homeless again. I'd never let myself live in places — or relationships — where I couldn't rest, where I couldn't be myself.

That promise became my fuel. Every setback, every tear, every long night of work — it was all part of honoring that vow.

There were moments I felt invisible, moments I doubted everything. I remember one night, working late, my hands aching, my body exhausted, and I whispered to myself, "You're doing this for a reason."

That reason became clearer over time. I wasn't just working for money — I was working for freedom. For dignity. For legacy.

And slowly, brick by brick, I built it.

When Success Feels Heavy

Here's something people don't talk about enough: sometimes, success feels just as heavy as struggle.

Because when you finally get what you prayed for — the business, the home, the stability — you realize it comes with new pressures. Everyone starts expecting more from you. Your time, your energy, your peace.

And as a woman who spent her whole life being the strong one, I found myself right back where I started — pouring into everyone else and forgetting to refill my own cup.

Until one day, I broke down. Not from failure, but from fatigue. From carrying too much, from being everything to everyone.

That's when I learned my next big lesson:

Rest is not a reward. It's a requirement.

You can't pour from an empty cup and expect abundance to overflow. I had to remind myself that I didn't come this far to burn out trying to keep everyone else comfortable.

So I started doing something radical — I started saying no.

No to people who drained me.

No to projects that didn't serve me.

No to the pressure to prove my worth.

And as soon as I did, peace found me again.

Redefining Strength

For most of my life, I thought strength meant never showing weakness. I thought it meant keeping my pain private, showing up with a smile even when I was breaking inside.

But now I see strength differently. Strength is not pretending you're okay — it's admitting when you're not and asking for help anyway.

It's giving yourself grace when you're learning. It's forgiving yourself for what you didn't know.

I used to be afraid of being seen as "soft." Now I know softness isn't weakness — it's balance. It's compassion. It's understanding your own limits.

True strength is being grounded in who you are — even when everything around you is uncertain.

Motherhood and Legacy

Motherhood changed me more than anything. My children gave me purpose, but they also mirrored my pain. Through them, I learned how much of my healing was necessary — not just for me, but for them.

Because kids don't just inherit your smile or your eyes — they inherit your patterns, your fears, your habits.

So I made a decision: the pain that raised me would not raise them.

That meant breaking cycles. It meant talking about emotions instead of silencing them. It meant apologizing when I was wrong. It meant showing them what healing looks like in real time.

THE LIFE OF DR. NICOLE SUTTON

I tell my kids often:

"You don't have to have it all figured out. You just have to keep moving forward." And I mean it — because that's what life really is: motion, evolution, grace.

The Woman I Became

There's a different kind of peace that comes when you realize you don't have to chase anyone or anything anymore.

The woman I am now doesn't move out of desperation. She moves out of direction.

I know now that I'm not in competition with anyone. My only competition is the woman I was yesterday.

I've learned that elevation requires separation. Not everyone is meant to go where you're going — and that's okay. Some people are lessons, not lifetimes.

I stopped taking it personally when people left. I stopped overexplaining myself to those who couldn't understand my journey.

THE LIFE OF DR. NICOLE SUTTON

Because I know now: those who are meant for me will align with me — not against me.

THE LIFE OF DR. NICOLE SUTTON

Faith My Process

Faith has been my anchor through it all. Even when I didn't understand what was happening, I learned to trust that it was working in my favor.

There were times I felt abandoned by God — like He was silent when I needed Him most. But later, I realized He was never gone. He was teaching me to depend on Him, not on people.

Faith doesn't always give you answers. Sometimes it just gives you peace in the waiting.

And looking back, I see that every delay was divine timing. Every rejection was redirection. Every fall was protection.

THE LIFE OF DR. NICOLE SUTTON

You might not see it while you're in the fire —

but one day you'll realize the fire didn't

destroy you. It refined you.

Purpose Over Popularity
In a world that chases likes, followers, and validation, I've learned to chase impact. Because being "seen" means nothing if you're not known for something real.

I want my story to mean something. I want my words to reach the woman sitting alone in her car, crying, thinking no one understands. I want her to know she's not alone — that this moment is not her ending, it's her awakening.

Purpose doesn't come from perfection. It comes from pain that's been transformed into power.

That's what I want people to see when they look at me — not just the success, but the journey that built it.

Peace, Not Performance
I used to wake up every day trying to prove myself. Now I wake up grateful.

Grateful that I can rest.

Grateful that I can provide.

Grateful that I survived what was meant to destroy me.

Because peace hits different when you've earned it. When you've cried for it. When you've fought your way through hell to find it.

These days, I no longer perform for approval. I move with purpose. I don't hustle for validation; I align with what fulfills me.

Because peace is not something you find outside yourself — it's something you protect within yourself.

How to Keep Going When Life Gets Hard

Here are some lessons I've learned through pain, perseverance, and purpose — truths that can help you hold on when you feel like letting go:

1. Turn your pain into purpose.

Don't run from your story — use it. What you've been through can help someone else heal. That's how you make meaning out of the hard things.

2. Stop waiting for the perfect time.

There is no perfect time — only now. Start where you are, with what you have, and trust that more will come once you move.

3. Protect your energy.

Not everyone deserves access to you. Protect your peace like your life depends on it — because it does.

4. Rest, but don't quit.

You can pause. You can cry. You can take a break. But promise yourself you won't give up. Even slow progress is progress.

5. Don't mistake delays for denial.

Sometimes the "not yet" is God's way of saying, I'm preparing something better.

6. Surround yourself with believers.

Find people who speak life into you, not doubt. Community is medicine. Isolation breeds fear.

7. Celebrate small wins.

Every step counts. You're not where you used to be, and that's something to be proud of.

8. Keep learning.

Growth doesn't stop once you "make it." Keep sharpening your mind and spirit. Evolve with your purpose.

9. Forgive yourself.

You did the best you could with what you knew. Now that you know better, do better — but do it with compassion.

10. Stay anchored in gratitude.

Even in the struggle, find one thing to be thankful for. Gratitude doesn't erase pain — it transforms perspective.

Just For YOU.
If you're reading this and you feel like your life is falling apart — please listen closely.

It's not falling apart. It's falling into place.

Every ending is a beginning in disguise.

Every delay is a detour meant to get you somewhere better.

Every failure is feedback for your next move.

You just have to keep going. Even when you can't see the light — keep walking. Because eventually, you'll realize you were the light the whole time.

You are not your past. You are not your pain.

THE LIFE OF DR. NICOLE SUTTON

You are the evidence that survival can turn into success, that broken pieces can still build beautiful things.

Keep walking. Keep believing. Keep building.

Because your story isn't over — it's only just beginning.

Chapter Four

Why I Keep Going
What keeps me going?

Honestly, it's a mix of so many things — but at the heart of it all is love. The love I have for my clients, my kids, my family, and myself.

There's nothing like the feeling I get when I satisfy a client — when they walk away with a smile, knowing I've given them more than just a service. I've given them confidence, joy, and a reason to come back. That alone fuels me more than I can explain. My work isn't just about service — it's about people. It's about connection. It's about impact.

Then there's my children. Watching them smile, seeing them live without knowing the struggle I had to go through — that's what gives me peace. I fight hard every day to give them a life where they never have to feel what I felt, never have to wonder where they'll sleep or how they'll eat. They don't have to carry that weight — I already carried it for them.

And now, there's someone else who keeps me pushing even harder — my grandson.

There's something about becoming a grandparent that shifts everything. He's a new heartbeat in my life, a fresh reason to take better care of myself. Every morning I wake up, stretch, and thank the universe for another chance to show up — for him. For my husband, who supports me and believes in me. For my family, who now sees a woman who rose above her past and became something greater.

For them, I stay focused. For them, I stay healthy. For them, I keep going. If there's one story from my life I want people to remember — it's this: Never give up.

I know that's something we hear all the time, but I'm living proof that those words carry power.

You can grind for five months straight — wondering if anything is working, wondering if your prayers are even being heard. Then bam! — one morning you wake up, and everything you've been dreaming of… starts happening.

That's how it happened for me.

THE LIFE OF DR. NICOLE SUTTON

I went from being homeless at 19, trying to survive, moving place to place, not knowing where my next meal would come from or where I'd sleep that night — to now running my own company, paying my own bills, and never having to ask anyone for help.

Do you know how empowering that feels?

I built a life out of what once felt like rubble. I turned pain into purpose. And if I can do that — so can you.

My story is not meant to impress you. It's meant to inspire you. It's meant to remind you that every setback is just the setup for your comeback.

THE LIFE OF DR. NICOLE SUTTON

You are reading the words of a woman who once had nothing. And now? I have everything that matters.

So let me be the voice that tells you — don't give up. Don't quit. Don't count yourself out just because life hasn't gone how you planned.

Your dream might be one more day away from coming true.

Keep building. Keep pushing. Keep believing.

Because if you refuse to give up, I promise — you will rise.

Sometimes, I still ask myself that question, "What keeps me going? Why am I not giving up despite all hardships I've been?" — not out of doubt, but reflection. Because when you've walked through as many storms as I have, you don't just move forward on autopilot. You move forward with intention. You wake up with gratitude. You remember what it felt like to be on the other side — the cold nights, the empty stomach, the quiet prayers whispered into the darkness — and you use that memory as fire.

I tell people all the time: success didn't come easy it didn't save me — hard work did. Hard work I did while thinking that one day all the pain would make sense, all the hardship will pay off. Hard work that even though it may take a wrong turn still would lead me where I was meant to be. I believe that my story would be more than just survival — it would be proof of transformation.

The Morning After Rock Bottom

Rock bottom doesn't look the same for everyone. For me, it was a silent morning sitting in my car with everything I owned packed in the back seat. I remember staring out the window, feeling small and invisible, wondering if this was it — if this was where my story ended.

But somewhere between the tears and exhaustion, something inside me shifted. I realized no one was coming to save me — and that wasn't a tragedy. It was freedom.

Because the moment you stop waiting for someone else to fix your life, you give yourself permission to rebuild it.

THE LIFE OF DR. NICOLE SUTTON

That morning, I promised myself that I would never let my circumstances define me again. I wasn't going to be another statistic, another "what could've been." I was going to rewrite my story, even if it meant starting from scratch.

And that's exactly what I did — one long, messy, beautiful chapter at a time.

The Climb That Changed Everything

The climb was slow. There were days I felt like I was making progress, and others where it seemed like I'd slid right back down. I worked long hours, juggling multiple jobs, taking classes, learning how to manage money, how to communicate, how to lead. I was building not just a business — but a mindset.

People often see the glow-up, but they rarely see the grind. They don't see the nights you cry quietly because you're scared but still show up the next day with a smile. They don't see you questioning yourself, wondering if you're strong enough, smart enough, or worthy enough to keep going.

But every small step, every late night, every sacrifice — it mattered. It was laying the foundation for something greater.

When my business started growing, it wasn't overnight. It was years of consistency, faith, and self-belief finally catching up to me. I poured my soul into every client, every project, every little detail — because I knew what it meant to feel unseen, and I never wanted anyone who crossed my path to feel that way.

The Power of Purpose

What drives me now is not just success — it's significance. I want to leave something behind that lasts longer than me. Something that reminds my kids, my grandson, and anyone watching that no matter where you start, you can rise.

Purpose is what turns pain into power. It's what transforms struggle into strength. When you know why you're doing something, you can endure almost anything.

That's what kept me going when I was exhausted, when business was slow, when doubt crept in. My why was always bigger than the "how." I didn't need to know how it would work out — I just needed to believe that it would.

And eventually, it did.

Becoming THE Example

When I look at my kids now, I see everything I fought for reflected in their eyes. They don't know the nights I spent crying in silence, the bills I worried about, the meals I skipped so they could eat. They just see stability. Safety. Love. And that's enough for me.

Then came my grandson — my beautiful reminder that life keeps giving new reasons to grow. His laughter fills the spaces that once held pain. His tiny hands remind me of why I must keep pushing to be the best version of myself. Because one day, when he's old enough to ask how I made it through, I want to tell him the truth — not a sugar-coated version, but the real, raw, honest truth.

That I failed, that I fell, that I cried — but I never stopped trying.

Because that's what legacy is. It's not the money you leave behind. It's the mindset. It's the faith. It's the example that tells the next generation, "If I could rise from nothing, so can you."

Love, the Quiet Fuel
If you ask me what love looks like now, I'd say it looks like showing up — every day — even when no one's clapping. It looks like pouring your heart into something you believe in. It looks like forgiving the past, including the version of yourself who didn't know better.

It looks like my husband holding my hand after a long day, reminding me that I'm not alone in this journey. It looks like my kids' laughter echoing through the house, my grandson's smile lighting up a room. That's love. That's purpose. That's life.

And I've learned something powerful: love isn't what keeps you from breaking — it's what helps you rebuild after you do.

The Reality Behind the Hustle

People see success and assume it's easy once you make it. But let me be real — it never gets easier. You just get stronger. You get wiser. You learn how to manage storms instead of avoiding them.

There are still days I doubt myself, days I feel overwhelmed, days I want to scream. But then I remember — I prayed for this. I fought for this. And I won't let temporary feelings make me forget permanent blessings.

Growth requires discomfort. You can't elevate and stay comfortable at the same time. I've learned to stop asking, "Why is this happening to me?" and start asking, "What is this teaching me?"

Because every challenge holds a lesson — and if you can stay long enough to learn it, you'll come out stronger than you ever imagined.

Redefining Success

I used to think success meant luxury, fame, and material things. But now, success feels quieter. It's peace of mind. It's freedom. It's being able to wake up without anxiety. It's being able to say no to things that don't align with your spirit. It's knowing that you're living your truth, not someone else's expectations.

I don't chase trends. I chase transformation — within myself and in the lives I touch. The real flex? Being happy. Being at peace. Being grateful.

Healing the Inner Child
There's still a little girl inside me — the one who wanted to be loved, seen, and safe. For a long time, I ignored her. I told her to toughen up, to keep moving, to survive. But as I healed, I realized she didn't need toughness — she needed tenderness.

So now, when I'm tired, I don't shame myself for resting. When I cry, I don't see it as weakness. When I feel afraid, I remind myself that fear is just faith in disguise — the part of me that still believes something greater is on the other side.

Healing isn't linear. It's messy. It's emotional. But it's worth it. Because once you start healing, you stop repeating. You stop settling. You start thriving.

Looking Forward

I don't know what the next five years will bring — and honestly, that doesn't scare me anymore. I've faced enough storms to know that I can handle whatever comes next.

My only goal now is to live fully, love deeply, and serve others through my story. To remind people that no matter how far they've fallen, there's still a way up.

Because if there's one truth I've learned, it's this: you don't have to have a perfect past to create a powerful future.

Every day is a second chance. Every sunrise is a new beginning. Every breath is proof that your story isn't over.

How to Keep Going When Life Gets Hard

If you're in a season of struggle, I want you to remember these truths. Write them down. Repeat them. Let them sink into your spirit.

1. You are not behind.

Everyone's journey moves at a different pace. Don't compare your chapter one to someone else's chapter twenty.

2. Your pain has purpose.

The things you've gone through weren't meant to break you — they were meant to shape you. Let your scars tell your story, not your shame.

3. Gratitude changes everything.

No matter how dark life feels, find one thing to be thankful for. Gratitude doesn't erase pain, but it softens it.

4. You can rest and still rise.

Taking a break doesn't mean you've failed. It means you're human. Even warriors need rest.

5. Protect your energy.

Don't pour into places that leave you empty. Peace is priceless — guard it fiercely.

6. Forgive yourself for surviving.

You did what you had to do to make it through. Stop punishing yourself for choices made in survival mode.

7. Keep showing up.

You might not see progress right away, but every step forward counts. Faith grows in motion.

8. Let go of who you used to be.

You can't step into your new life while clinging to your old self. Release what no longer fits your spirit.

9. Don't be afraid to ask for help.

Strength doesn't mean doing everything alone. It's knowing when to lean on others.

10. Believe again.

Even if life has disappointed you — trust again. Love again. Dream again. Because hope is what heals us.

Just For YOU.
I'm still learning. Still growing. Still becoming.

But one thing I know for sure — I will never give up.

And I hope, after reading this, you won't either.

Because even when life feels heavy, even when you can't see the end of the tunnel, keep walking.

Your light is waiting on the other side.

You've made it through 100% of your worst days — and that means you're already stronger than you think.

So don't stop now. Keep going. Keep believing. Keep building.

THE LIFE OF DR. NICOLE SUTTON

Your rise is coming — and when it does, you'll look back and realize every storm was worth it.

Chapter Five

Becoming the Brand

There was a moment when I realized I wasn't just doing a job anymore—I was building something bigger. I was becoming a brand. That shift in mindset changed everything.

The first thing I did was take it seriously: I officially set up my business, completed all the necessary paperwork, and invested in professional software. None of this came cheap. I paid thousands of dollars for training and certifications. Most importantly, I hired a top tier mentor—someone who had already been where I wanted to go.

Having the right mentor made a world of difference. They kept me accountable, made sure I took the right classes, attended the right boot camps, and followed the steps that would lead me toward excellence. I knew if I wanted a high-quality business, I needed high-quality guidance. That investment in mentorship was the foundation of my brand.

Then came the moment that sealed it: I received my first official paycheck from my business. I couldn't believe my eyes. It was real. The work I had done, the classes I had taken, the long hours I had put in—all of it had brought me to that moment. That day, my brand was born.

Becoming The Vision

There was a time when I used to dream about success like it was a faraway place — something reserved for other people. But once I began building my business and putting structure behind my goals, I realized success wasn't a destination. It was a decision. It was something I could choose to live, breathe, and build every single day.

When I got that first official paycheck, I cried — not because of the money, but because of what it meant. It meant that everything I had endured, every night I spent questioning myself, had led to this. It wasn't luck. It was work. It was faith. It was proof that what I'd prayed for was finally meeting what I'd prepared for.

THE LIFE OF DR. NICOLE SUTTON

That moment didn't just confirm my purpose

— it redefined it.

From "Rich Girl" to WhiteApple Financial

Originally, my company was called The Rich Girl Brand LLC. That name meant everything to me—it reflected my journey, my ambition, and my identity. But when I tried to take it to the next level, I ran into resistance. Some banks didn't like the word rich in the name, and the income I was bringing in seemed to raise eyebrows because I was doing it alone and they don't believe it.

So I pivoted. I rebranded. In 2025, WhiteApple Financial was born. That name, too, holds deep personal meaning. And while The Rich Girl Brand will always be my first baby, WhiteApple Financial is now the foundation for everything I'm building. It represents evolution, growth, and maturity.

The Evolution of a Brand

When I started The Rich Girl Brand, it wasn't just a business name — it was my declaration to the world that I was no longer playing small. That name represented the girl who came from nothing and still dared to dream big. "Rich" wasn't just about money. It was about mindset, abundance, and self-worth.

But as the business grew, I faced new challenges. I started running into doors that wouldn't open — not because I wasn't qualified, but because of how people perceived me. Banks didn't like the word "Rich." Some people assumed I was being flashy. They didn't understand that it was never about ego — it was about empowerment.

Still, I learned something powerful: sometimes evolution requires separation. So I rebranded.

WhiteApple Financial was born out of maturity — out of clarity. The name "WhiteApple" symbolizes purity, balance, and growth. It represents a clean slate, a new chapter, and the confidence to stand on my own terms.

That transition wasn't easy. It meant starting fresh, reintroducing myself to the world, and rebuilding trust in a new identity. But it also showed me that true power doesn't come from a name — it comes from the integrity behind it.

And from that moment forward, I told myself: Every decision I make will be rooted in integrity, not image

Lesson learned: when you're in the finance industry, perception matters. A name like Rich Girl can be misunderstood. So I adjusted — and it was one of the best moves I made.

Starting a Business from Nothing

If you're starting a business with nothing, my advice is simple:

Don't give up.

Make sure it's something you're willing to do for free — because in the beginning, you probably will.

Be willing to take classes. Get a mentor. Work under someone else in the field first if you have to. Test it out. Volunteer. Shadow somebody. See if it's really what you want before you pour your time, money, and energy into it. And most of all — prepare to sacrifice. You're going to give up a lot in the beginning. But it's worth it.

Build relationships. Network with others in your industry. Ask questions. Stay curious. Learn how to stand on your own feet. Your connections can open doors that hard work alone can't.

Handling Business, Not Hustling

People love to talk about hustling. But in my world, I don't use that word. Hustling sounds like cutting corners or rushing through things. That's not how I run WhiteApple Financial.

I don't hustle my business. I handle it.

Handling your business means making sure your clients are cared for, not just processed. It means aiming for a 95% satisfaction rate, even though you know you can't please everyone. It means treating people with respect and giving them your best, every time.

That's the difference. Hustling is short-term. Handling business is long-term. And I'm here for the long haul.

Professionalism: The Language of Success

The deeper I went into entrepreneurship, the more I realized something — professionalism will take you places talent can't.

You can have the best service, the best idea, the best skill — but if your communication, consistency, or attitude doesn't match, people won't stay. In business, you're not just selling a product or a service; you're selling trust.

That's why WhiteApple Financial was built on three core values:

Security. Integrity. Professionalism.

Those aren't just words we print on our website — they're principles we live by.

Because I've learned that how you make people feel will determine how far your business goes. Clients might forget what you said or did, but they will never forget how you made them feel.

At WhiteApple, I teach my team that every phone call, every message, every appointment is an opportunity to build trust. You can't fake that kind of care — it has to come from within.

Integrity is what you do when no one's watching. Professionalism is how you do it. And consistency? That's how you prove it.

From Hustling to Handling Business

People love to romanticize "the hustle." But truthfully, I don't hustle anymore.

To me, hustling sounds chaotic — like moving fast without a clear direction. I don't hustle my business. I handle it.

Handling business means you move with structure. You move with strategy. You don't chase every opportunity — you choose the right ones.

There's a difference between motion and progress. Hustlers move a lot; handlers move with purpose.

When you're handling your business, you're not just trying to survive — you're building something that can sustain. Something that can stand without you. That's the kind of legacy I'm building.

Because I don't just want to make money — I want to make meaning.

Sacrifice and Self-Mastery

Entrepreneurship will test everything in you. Your patience. Your emotions. Your discipline. Your faith.

There were nights when I barely slept — nights when I wanted to quit, when I questioned if I was strong enough. But every time I felt like giving up, I reminded myself of that young woman who once slept in her car. I reminded myself that I made a promise — I will never go back.

That promise keeps me focused. It keeps me grateful.

I learned to say no to short-term pleasures for long-term peace. I turned down parties, vacations, and countless "fun" moments because I was busy building something that would last.

Success demands sacrifice — but not forever. Just long enough for you to get where you're going.

And once you arrive, you realize that the peace you gain from being disciplined is worth far more than anything you gave up.

The Weight of Responsibility
Leadership came faster than I expected. One day, I was just trying to keep my business afloat; the next, I had people looking to me for guidance. And let me tell you — leadership is not for the faint of heart.

When you're a leader, every move matters. Every word carries weight. Every decision ripples out into someone else's life. You have to lead with confidence even when you're scared, and sometimes you have to walk alone before anyone understands your vision.

I learned quickly that leadership doesn't mean being perfect. It means being present. It means being humble enough to learn and strong enough to stand tall when the world tries to knock you down.

There were days I questioned if I was cut out for it. I'd hear whispers — "She thinks she's better now," "She changed," "Who does she think she is?"

At first, those words stung. I used to take them personally. But one day, I realized something: people will always talk. Whether you're doing bad or doing good, someone will always have something to say. And once I accepted that, I found peace.

Because while they were talking, I was building.

While they were doubting, I was learning.

While they were watching, I was working.

And that's what separates a dreamer from a doer.

The Reality of Growth
Growth can be lonely.

When you start elevating, not everyone will come with you. Some people will distance themselves. Some will envy you. Others will misunderstand your heart.

But I learned not to take it personally. Because everyone's not meant to understand your vision — it wasn't given to them.

You will outgrow environments, conversations, and even relationships. And that's okay. Growth isn't betrayal — it's alignment.

The higher you go, the quieter it gets. But in that silence, you'll find clarity. And once you start walking in purpose, peace becomes your

new success metric.

Legacy Over Lifestyle
At this stage of my life, I'm not chasing luxury — I'm building legacy.

Legacy means my kids won't have to start where I started. It means they'll inherit systems, structure, and strength. It means my grandson will know that his grandmother didn't just build a business — she built a blueprint.

I want my name to represent resilience. I want people to hear "WhiteApple Financial" and know it stands for trust, integrity, and empowerment.

Because what good is success if it doesn't open doors for others?

THE LIFE OF DR. NICOLE SUTTON

True legacy is when you plant trees under whose shade you may never sit.

The Woman Behind the Brand

Sometimes people see the business, the clients, the brand — but they forget there's a woman behind it all. A woman who's still growing, still healing, still learning.

I'm proud of the businesswoman I've become. But I'm even prouder of the woman I am becoming — one who leads with compassion, walks with grace, and lives with purpose.

Because no amount of success matters if I lose myself in the process.

So I take time now to rest, reflect, and reconnect with my "why." To celebrate not just the wins, but the journey. Because the journey itself — every detour, every breakdown, every lesson — that's where beauty really is.

Lessons for Those Ready to Build Something from Nothing

If my story teaches you anything, let it be this: you can start over and still win. Here are some truths that guided me — and maybe they'll guide you too:

1. Believe in your vision before anyone else does.

You don't need validation to begin. You just need courage. Your dream doesn't have to make sense to anyone but you.

2. Start where you are — with what you have.

Perfection is a trap. Use what's in your hands, and more will come as you grow.

3. Treat your business like it's already a brand.

Professionalism starts before the profit. Build structure before success shows up.

4. Invest in mentorship.

A good mentor will show you what shortcuts can't. Learn from those who've already built what you're dreaming of.

5. Don't chase clout — chase clarity.

Popularity fades. Purpose doesn't.

6. Rebrand without fear.

Sometimes growth requires change. Don't be afraid to evolve into your next level.

7. Don't hustle — handle your business.

Move with strategy, not chaos. Progress isn't about how fast you go — it's about how well you build.

8. Keep your integrity at all costs.

The way you treat people is your real business card. Be the same person behind closed doors as you are in public.

9. Learn to detach from opinions.

Not everyone will understand your journey — and that's okay. Walk in purpose anyway.

10. Build for legacy, not lifestyle.

The goal isn't just to live well — it's to leave something behind that lasts.

Just for YOU.

If there's one thing I've learned through it all, it's that growth never stops. Every level comes with new lessons. But that's the beauty of it — you keep evolving, you keep learning, you keep rising.

I used to dream of a day when I'd finally "make it."

Now, I understand — I already have.

Because success isn't a destination. It's waking up every day with gratitude, purpose, and peace.

It's knowing that everything you went through wasn't in vain — it built the strength you stand on now.

So to anyone reading this, wondering if it's too late, too hard, or too big — listen to me:

You are capable.

You are chosen.

And your vision is valid.

Keep going. Build it. Believe in it. Become it.

Because one day, you'll look back and realize you weren't just building a business —

you were becoming the woman you were always meant to be.

Chapter Six

The Power of Saying No

For a long time, I was what people would call a "yes girl."

I said yes to everything — to everyone. I helped people every month without hesitation. If someone called needing money, advice, a ride, or even just my time, I was there. I was the dependable one. The helper. The problem solver.

But over time, I started to notice something: the moment I stopped saying yes, the same people I had poured into began to act different. They got quiet. Distant. Some even got mad. That was my turning point.

THE LIFE OF DR. NICOLE SUTTON

I realized if people would turn on me just because I said "no" once or twice, maybe I should have said "no" from the beginning.

It hurt, but it was eye-opening. I had built so many one-sided relationships — ones where I gave and gave, but the moment I needed something, there was silence. And that silence taught me something powerful: not everyone deserves your yes.

When I first started setting boundaries, I thought I was going to lose people — and I did. But what I didn't expect was how much of myself I would find in the process.

You see, when you spend years saying yes to everyone else, you slowly start saying no to yourself. You forget what you want, what you need, and what you deserve. You become a supporting character in other people's stories — always showing up, always giving, always pouring — until you wake up one day completely drained.

I remember sitting at my desk one evening, phone buzzing with messages, and realizing something had to change. I wasn't living — I was managing chaos. I wasn't at peace — I was surviving.

So I made a decision that scared me but also set me free:

I would stop performing and start protecting.

And that's when my real transformation began.

When "No" Becomes Your Superpower
Saying no used to feel selfish.

Now, it feels sacred.

At first, people didn't understand. They thought I was being cold, distant, or too focused on myself. What they didn't see was the exhaustion behind my smile — the silent frustration that came from always being everything for everyone.

When I started saying no, I got pushback. Some people stopped calling. Some got offended. But over time, something beautiful happened — I started attracting people who respected my boundaries. People who didn't take my energy, but matched it. People who didn't call only when they needed something,

but just to check in.

That's the magic of "no."

It clears the room for what's real.

THE LIFE OF DR. NICOLE SUTTON

The Year of Tough Love - 2025
This year, 2025, became the year I had to start practicing tough love. I used to think being nice meant saying yes. But I've learned that real love — for others and for yourself — means setting limits.

It's funny how you can be cool with so many people, how you can give and show up for them, but the moment you need something, you start looking around like, "Who can I really call?" And the truth? Sometimes the answer is no one.

That realization hit me hard. I told myself, I refuse to go back to where I started from — that place of struggle and instability. Remember, I promised myself I would never be homeless again.

So I had to toughen up. I had to help myself first before helping everyone else. I stopped handing out favors like candy. I stopped letting people drain my time, money, and energy. I stopped getting "pimped," as I like to call it, because that's exactly what it felt like — being used in the name of kindness.

Now, instead of giving handouts, I give with intention. I decided if I'm going to spend $500 a month, it's going to feed the homeless — the people who truly need it. I don't ask for donations. I don't wait for sponsors. If my heart says feed them, I take it out of my own pocket. That's my calling, and I honor it.

Other people may see it differently, and that's okay. But for me, it feels good knowing I'm helping people who don't expect anything in return — people who are grateful, not entitled.

Because in this world, if you don't look out for yourself, no one will. Your husband or wife might, but that's about it. Think about it — your mom loved you because she brought you into this world. Your siblings love you because you share blood. But your spouse? They chose you. And that kind of love, the kind that's chosen, is sacred.

That's the kind of loyalty I want in my life — mutual, chosen, and respected. '

ABOUT THE AUTHOR

Dr. Nicole Sutton is an entrepreneur, business owner, and transformational storyteller whose work centers on resilience, personal growth, and empowerment. Known for her authenticity and lived-experience insight, she built her career by turning adversity into opportunity and purpose.

After overcoming homelessness, financial instability, and generational challenges, Dr. Sutton went on to found **WhiteApple Financial Company**, formerly known as Rich Girl Brand LLC. Her work reflects a commitment to helping others navigate life transitions with clarity, accountability, and confidence. Through business, mentorship, and service-based leadership, she continues to inspire individuals to reclaim control of their lives and futures.

As an author, Dr. Sutton uses storytelling as a tool for healing and connection. Her writing speaks to women who have faced hardship and are ready to move from survival into stability. *The Life of Dr. Nicole Sutton* is her debut memoir and a reflection of her belief that pain, when processed with intention, can become purpose.

THE LIFE OF DR. NICOLE SUTTON

www.ingramcontent.com/pod-product-compliance
Lightning Source LLC
Chambersburg PA
CBHW060836190426
43197CB00040B/2639